A journey down the Thames

The River Thames is one of the most famous rivers in the world.
As we travel down the Thames we see reminders of every period
of British history.

Although the River Thames is famous it is not very long.
It is tiny when compared with rivers like the Nile and the Amazon.
But it flows through a great capital city – London.
It is also a great industrial waterway.

River Journeys

A journey down the Thames

Laurie Bolwell

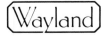

River Journeys

A journey up the Amazon
A journey down the Danube
A journey down the Ganges
A journey down the Mississippi
A journey up the Nile
A journey down the Rhine
A journey down the Seine
A journey down the Thames

*This book is based on an
original text by Charles Lyte*

Some words in this book are printed
in **bold**. Their meanings are explained
in the glossary on page 64.

First published in 1984 by
Wayland (Publishers) Ltd
49 Lansdowne Place, Hove
East Sussex BN3 1HF, England

© Copyright 1984 Wayland (Publishers) Ltd

ISBN 0 85078 406 9

Phototypeset by Kalligraphics Ltd, Redhill, Surrey
Printed in Italy by G. Canale & C.S.p.A., Turin
Bound in the UK by R. J. Acford, Chichester

Contents

The Thames in the Past

Here are the first animals and
men to live along the Thames.
The climate was colder then.
The men are dressed in furs.
They hunted animals for food.
This is how they would try to
kill a giant **mammoth**.

At the end of the **Ice Age**
England was joined to Europe.
The Thames was then joined to
the River Rhine.

Stone Age people came to the Thames valley from Europe.
They hunted elephants, oxen, deer, and fished in the river.
Much later the Celts lived along the Thames.
Then came the Romans who built the first London Bridge.
Many old bridges can still be seen like the one above.

There are old customs found
along the River Thames.
Here is one.
It is called swan-upping.
Men go up the river by boat.
They count the swans they find.

After the Romans left other
invaders sailed up the Thames.
The Anglo-Saxons came to rob.
They came in the 5th century.

Some 500 years later in 1066
the Normans came to England.

Since 1066 there have been no
more invaders.

Here is the port of London about 200 years ago.
You can tell the port is very busy from all the ships.
Big ships can travel 50 miles up the Thames from the sea.
So London is a very safe sheltered port.

Goods were brought to London from all over the country.
Many of the goods were exported to the rest of the world.
In olden days goods were carried to London in carts.
About 200 years ago **canals** were cut.
Here is the Regent's Canal in London.
The **barges** have travelled from Manchester to London.

This is the Chelsea **embankment** at the time of Queen Victoria.
The embankment made London safer from flooding by the Thames.

13

The Thames sometimes froze over.
Fairs were held on the ice.

This is a big houseboat moored on the River Thames near London.

At one time goods were carried by sailing barges. Here are three old barges on show on the Thames. These old barges race on the river to remind people of what the river used to be like.

From the Source to Reading

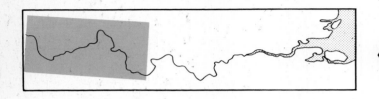

Here is a map of the Thames. The blue shows the section from the **source** to Reading.

The River Thames starts in Gloucestershire in a **spring**.
The spring is called Thames Head and is the source of the river.

This is Seven Springs which is the source of the River Churn.
The Churn is a **tributary** of the Thames.
At one time many people thought Seven Springs was the source of the River Thames.
In 1937 Parliament decided that Thames Head was its source.

Early-morning fishermen on the Thames.

Locks have been built to make the river navigable.
Here is Goring Lock which is a famous beauty spot.
The level of water is controlled by the lock.
This allows boats to move up and down the river.

Apart from London the greatest city on the Thames is Oxford.
Oxford is one of the most famous university cities.
These are some of the Oxford colleges.

Students at Oxford enjoy the
River Thames.
They can sit and read on the
river-banks.
Rowing is an important sport.
Punting is for fun.
Punts are boats with flat
bottoms.
Here are some people in
a punt on the river.

The flow of water in the river is also controlled by **weirs**.
This is Pangbourne Weir.

In the past the river also provided power for mills.
This is the village of Whitchurch which had watermills.
The high building was once a mill.

Henley to Teddington

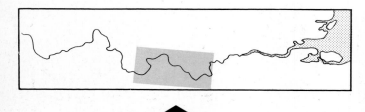

The next section of the river is shown on the map.

People who live along the river need bridges to cross. This is the bridge at Marlow. It was the first **suspension bridge** to be built.

This is Henley an attractive market town.
Henley is famous for its rowing **regatta** which started in 1839.

Although many people now live along the river the banks are still unspoiled in many places.

This is the most famous view on this part of the river.
It is Windsor Castle, the home of the Royal family.
The castle is the largest castle in England.

This is another famous tourist attraction on the
banks of the River Thames.
It is Hampton Court which was a palace of King Henry VIII.
It was built 450 years ago by Cardinal Wolsey.
King Henry VIII took it from him when the Cardinal fell
from royal favour.

This is Teddington Lock.
The weir is a famous landmark.

The river here is about 76
metres (250 feet) wide.
The weir marks the spot where
fresh water flowing down the
Thames meets **tidal water.**

Richmond to Putney

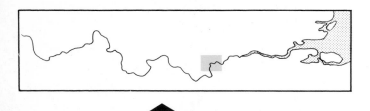

This is a short but important stretch of the River Thames.

King Charles I made a royal hunting ground at Richmond. It is now Richmond Park. It has deer in it.

Here is the River Thames at Richmond.
You can hire rowing boats there to explore the river.

This is Brentford Dock where the Grand Union Canal ends.
This canal links Birmingham with London.
Many working boats once used the canal but few do so now.

Around a big loop in the river beyond Richmond is Kew.
Kew Gardens has plants from all over the world.
Here are giant water lilies growing in a hothouse at Kew.
These water lilies came from the River Amazon in Brazil.

Here is the University Boat
Race between Oxford and
Cambridge Universities.
Many people watch the race
from the bridges and banks.

The places along the river
have changed in character.
Chiswick **Quay** was once a canal
basin where barges moored.
Now it has been cleaned up.
New homes have been built
around the canal basin.

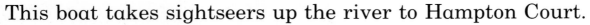

This boat takes sightseers up the river to Hampton Court.

The River Thames provides water for Londoners.
These are reservoirs at Barn Elms near Hammersmith Bridge.

London

Here is the River Thames near Cheyne Walk in Chelsea.
The houseboats are moored here all the time.
Some people prefer living on the river to living in a house.

This is a map of the River Thames in London.
You can see how many historic places are near the river.

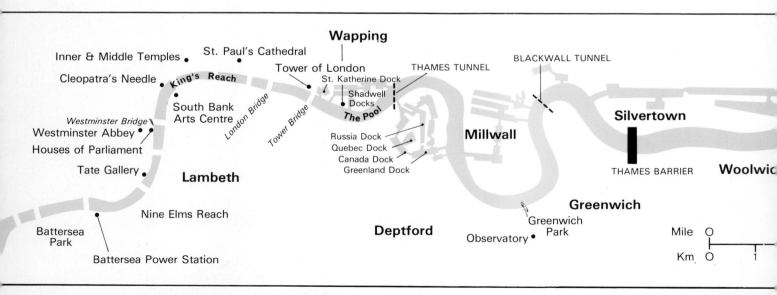

Look at the map on page 40 again.
Find the Houses of Parliament and Lambeth.
This picture was taken from Lambeth across the river.

The Houses of Parliament are not as old as they look.
The present buildings were finished in 1860.
They were badly damaged in the Second World War (1939–45).
Bombs were dropped on Parliament by German bombers.
After the war it was restored to how it had been before.

Here is the best-known
landmark in London.
It is Big Ben.
Find it on the picture opposite.

At the end of the war much of London had to be repaired or rebuilt.
In 1951 the Festival of Britain was held on the South Bank.
It was a festival to celebrate getting back to normal.
After the Festival a concert hall was built on the land.
This is the Royal Festival Hall which can hold 3,000 people.

These scientists are examining
fish caught in the Thames.
They are checking for signs
of **pollution**.
The river is much cleaner
than it used to be.
Nearly 100 different types of
fish live in the river now.

You will see this **obelisk** on
the Embankment.
It is more than 3,000 years old.
It is called Cleopatra's Needle.
It was made in ancient Egypt.
In 1819 it was presented to
England by the King of Egypt.
It was put in a cylinder and
towed there behind a ship.

When the Thames flows alongside the ancient City of London
it passes many other famous sights.
Here you can see St. Paul's Cathedral which was built in 1666
after the Great Fire of London.

Look at the map on page 40 and find St. Paul's Cathedral.
Part of the river near St. Paul's is called King's Reach.
The famous Inns of Court, the law centres of London, are here.

In the past the south bank of the river opposite St. Paul's
was famous for theatres, like these two.
This is where Shakespeare once had his Globe Theatre.

The Romans built the first bridge over the Thames in London.
Other bridges were later built at the same spot.
Since this was the only crossing it was called London Bridge.
The earliest bridges were built of wood.
In 1176 a strong stone bridge was built.
It lasted for 600 years and this is how it looked.

There were houses and shops on the bridge.
It had a spiked gateway on which the heads of executed traitors
were displayed as a warning to others.
Look at the picture and you can see heads on spikes.

In 1831 a new bridge had to be built.
In 1967 London Bridge had to be widened.
The outside stones were taken down, sold for 2½
million dollars and taken to Arizona in America.
They were used to make a 'new' London Bridge.

The Tower of London is a great treasure house.

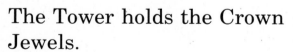
The Tower holds the Crown Jewels.
These men guard the Tower.
They are called beefeaters.

Here is Traitor's Gate.
It leads to the dungeons.

From the Docks to the Sea

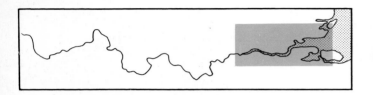

The last section of the River Thames begins at Tower Bridge. It is the dockland area.

This is Tower Bridge, the last bridge on the Thames.
The bridge has been lifted for the tall ship to pass through.

The docks of London are now not used for trade.
Old docks have been put to new uses.
This is St. Katherine's Dock.
There is a ship museum there.
Here are some historic ships.

This picture is a cross-section of the River Thames in Victorian times.

It shows the Thames Tunnel. It was the first underwater tunnel built to walk through. It took 11 years to build.

It was opened in 1843. Today it is used by underground trains.

Downstream is Greenwich.
Famous ships are docked there.
Here is the Cutty Sark.
It was a fast tea clipper.

In Greenwich Park you can see
the old Royal Observatory.
All lines of **latitude** are
measured from here.

London has suffered many floods in its history.
The picture above shows the new Thames Barrier
being built.
The Barrier is able to keep out the very high tides which
endanger the city, so London is now much safer.

In the past when the River Thames broke its banks scenes like this were common.
Some of the people in the picture seem to be enjoying it.

↑

A new port has been built at Tilbury to handle **containers**.
Here is an ocean-going container ship moving downstream.

Towards the mouth of the river the banks of the Thames are flat.
At one time this was an empty area of marshland.
Now there have been many modern developments here.
This is part of Thamesmead, a new town for 50,000 people.

59

This is part of the **estuary** of
the River Thames.

Here are mudflats off the
Isle of Grain.
An oil tanker is leaving the
Shellhaven refinery.

Sea birds like this herring
gull live in the emptier areas.

This is a power station opposite Sheerness.
Land in the estuary has been used for industries which need
huge amounts of water.

Ships from all over the world bring oil to this refinery
on the Isle of Grain.

Glossary

Barge   A flat-bottomed cargo boat used on canals and rivers.

Basin   A dock with lock gates.

Canal   Artificial watercourse used to carry goods and people.

Container   A large crate in which goods are packed for transporting by ship or lorry.

Embankment   Bank or mound to control water.

Estuary   Wide river mouth into which tides flow.

Ice Age   A period of tens of thousands of years ago when Britain was covered by ice.

Latitude   The distance of a place north or south of the equator

Lock   Gates across a canal or river to change water level.

Mammoth   A large extinct elephant.

Obelisk   A stone monument shaped like a needle.

Pollution   When land, air or water is made unclean and unhealthy, it is said to be polluted.

Quay   A landing place where ships unload or load cargoes.

Regatta   A series of races for boats.

Source   Where a river begins.

Spring   Stream of water coming to the surface from underground.

Suspension bridge   A bridge held up by cables that hang between two towers.

Tidal   Part of a river where water level changes with the tides.

Tributary   Stream or a river which flows into a larger river.

Weir   Dam or barrier built to control water level and flow.

Index

Picture acknowledgements

The illustrations in this book were supplied by: Aerofilms Library *cover, frontispiece*, 26, 27; British Tourist Authority 22, 32, 36–7, 50 (right); J. Allan Cash 9, 19, 21, 25, 28, 29, 31, 34, 35, 39, 41, 42, 46, 50 (top left), 51, 55 (top left), 58, 60, 62, 63; Handford Photography 56; Eric Hosking 10, 61 (bottom left); Mansell Collection 11, 47; Archie Miles 23; Popperfoto 16, 17, 24, 30, 33, 38, 43, 44, 45 (bottom right); TOPHAM 20. Illustrations on pages 8, 12, 13, 14–15, 48, 54 and 57 are from the Wayland Picture Library. Artwork by Alan Gunston.

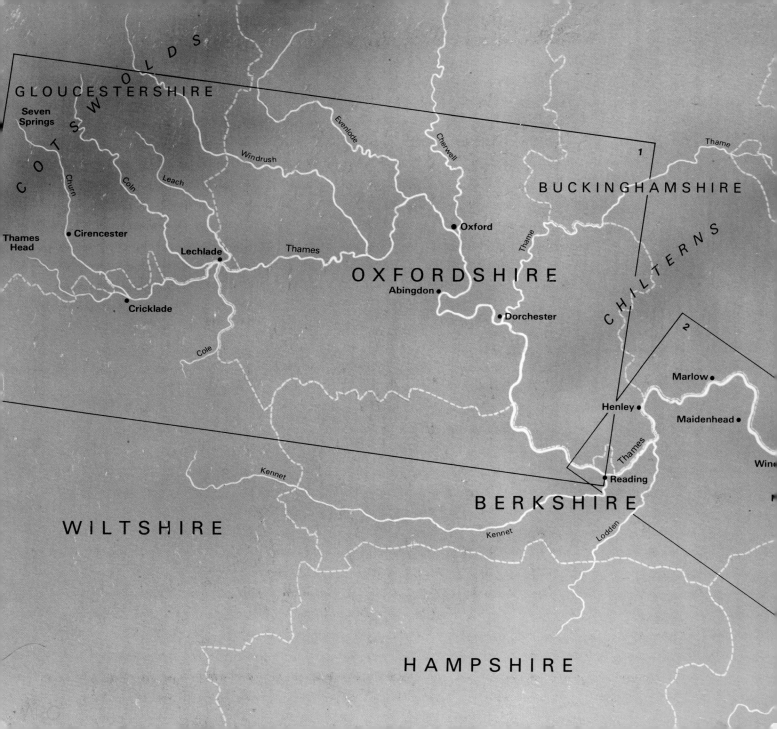